GLENDALE
91..13127

W9-BQD-078

GLENDALE MEDIA CENTER

WONDERFUL WORLD OF ANIMALS

For a free color catalog describing Gareth Stevens' list of high-quality books and multimedia programs, call 1-800-542-2595 (USA) or 1-800-461-9120 (Canada). Gareth Stevens Publishing's Fax: (414) 225-0377.
See our catalog, too, on the World Wide Web: http://gsinc.com

Library of Congress Cataloging-in-Publication Data

MacLeod, Beatrice.
    Reptiles / text by Beatrice MacLeod ; illustrated by Umberta Pezzuoli.
      p. cm. -- (Wonderful world of animals)
    Includes bibliographical references (p. 31) and index.
    Summary: Introduces the physical characteristics, behavior, and habitat of various reptiles.
    ISBN 0-8368-1958-6 (lib. bdg.)
    1. Reptiles--Juvenile literature. [1. Reptiles.] I. Pezzuoli, Umberta, ill.
II. Title. III. Series : MacLeod, Beatrice. Wonderful world of animals.
QL644.2.M3135 1997
597.9--dc21   97-20188

This North American edition first published in 1997 by
Gareth Stevens Publishing
1555 North RiverCenter Drive, Suite 201
Milwaukee, Wisconsin 53212 USA

This U.S. edition © 1997 by Gareth Stevens, Inc. Created and produced with original © 1996 by McRae Books Srl, Via dei Rustici, 5 - Florence, Italy. Additional end matter © 1997 by Gareth Stevens, Inc.

Text: Beatrice MacLeod
Design: Marco Nardi
Illustrations: Umberta Pezzuoli
U.S. Editor: Patricia Lantier-Sampon
Editorial assistants: Diane Laska, Rita Reitci

Note: Beatrice MacLeod has a Bachelor of Science degree in Biology. She works as a freelance journalist for Italian nature magazines and also writes children's nonfiction books on nature.

All rights reserved. No part of this book may be reproduced, stored in a retrieval system, or transmitted in any form or by any means, electronic, mechanical, photocopying, or otherwise, without the prior written permission of the copyright holder.

Printed in the United States of America

1 2 3 4 5 6 7 8 9 01 00 99 98 97

WONDERFUL WORLD OF ANIMALS

REPTILES

Text by Beatrice MacLeod
Illustrations by Umberta Pezzuoli

597.9
MAC

BC# 36313 0111 9880 6 Call # MAC

Gareth Stevens Publishing
MILWAUKEE

WHAT IS A REPTILE?

Reptiles include crocodiles, turtles, snakes, and lizards. All reptiles have scales and breathe through their lungs. Unlike birds and mammals, which have constant body temperatures, a reptile adapts its temperature to the environment in which it lives.

Tortoises and **turtles** have hard shells to protect their bodies. The hard topside, or shield, is rounded and attached to the soft, flat underside. Their toothless mouths have a cutting bony ridge that is as sharp as a beak.

Atlantic sea turtle

Crocodiles spend most of their lives in water. They use their tails to swim. They have long snouts and strong jaws with sharp teeth to catch unsuspecting prey.

Nile crocodile

Snakes have long, slender bodies covered in a scaly skin. They can measure from 8 inches (20 centimeters) to 33 feet (10 meters) in length. Most snakes have poor eyesight; they recognize other animals by vibrations on the ground or by smell.

Leopard snake

MOVEMENT

The word *reptile* comes from Latin and means "crawling." Snakes have no legs, and they slither along the ground. But many reptiles can also swim, run, or even glide through the air!

Tortoises have short toes for walking on land. Aquatic turtles have long toes with webbing for swimming.

Matamata

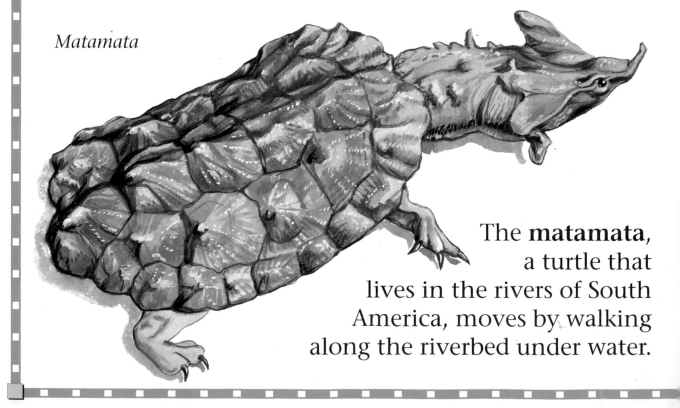

The **matamata**, a turtle that lives in the rivers of South America, moves by walking along the riverbed under water.

The **flying dragon**, a small Southeast Asian lizard, is one of the few reptiles that can "fly."

Flying dragon

By opening out a thin fold of skin along the sides of its body, it can glide from perch to perch up to 45 feet (14 m).

Speed

Speed is useful for defense and hunting. The tortoise moves very slowly, but it is a patient hunter and has a protective shell. In the water, some turtles can speed along at 18 miles (29 kilometers) per hour! The race runner lizard in America was also timed at this speed.

LAND REPTILES

Most reptiles live in Earth's warm tropical areas. Many also live in cooler temperate zones. Generally speaking, the number of reptiles decreases as you move farther away from the equator.

The **Australian frilled lizard** lives in the arid grasslands of Australia. When threatened by a predator, it sets up a collar of skin around its neck, making it look much bigger and scarier than it actually is.

Australian frilled lizard

Huge, heavy, and slow-moving, the **Galápagos giant tortoise** lives on the islands of *Galápagos* (a Spanish word meaning "tortoise") in the Pacific Ocean. They originally came from South America.

Galápagos giant tortoise

Emerald boa

The **emerald boa** lives in the tropical rain forests of South America. It lies in wait for prey in the trees, almost invisible against the green leaves. This boa is not poisonous, but kills its prey with its huge front fangs.

Aquatic Reptiles

Many reptiles, including sea turtles, crocodiles, many snakes, and large lizards like the marine iguana, live and feed mainly in the water. However, like almost all reptiles, they breed on land.

The **gavial**, a feared predator of the great rivers of India, is a species of crocodile. It has a long, thin snout with sharp pointed teeth, which it uses to catch fish.

Gavial

Many snakes can swim, but only a few can stay in the water for any length of time. The **sea krait** is a typical sea snake. It has valvelike closings on its nostrils, and its tissues extract oxygen from the water. It does not come ashore, but has live young at sea.

Sea krait

Endangered reptiles

Despite their ferocious reputations, many species of crocodiles and alligators are threatened. Their skins, as well as turtle shells and monitor lizard skins, are valuable for making shoes, belts, bags, wallets, and other fashion accessories.

FOOD AND FEEDING

Only a few iguana species and some land tortoises are plant-eaters. All other reptiles are carnivores. This means they eat meat, including birds, frogs, insects, fish, other reptiles, and even large mammals. Some snake species can swallow prey much larger than themselves.

The **marine iguana** is a large lizard that lives on the Galápagos Islands. It dives into the water to feed on algae and has special nose glands to excrete excess salt.

Marine iguana

Alligator snapping turtle

Alligator snapping turtles

hunt on the bottoms of rivers and lakes.
Their dark shells blend in perfectly with the
muddy bottoms and weeds. When fishing,
they open their mouth and wait, attracting
prey by means of a wormlike lure near their
tongue. Fish swim right into their mouth.

Age and size — some reptile records
The Asian saltwater crocodile is the largest reptile in
the world. Males grow up to 16 feet (5 m) long and
weigh over 1,000 pounds (453 kilograms). Tortoises
live the longest among reptiles; many species live
over 100 years. The oldest tortoise died at age 152.

HUNTING TECHNIQUES

Snakes, crocodiles, lizards, and even slow-moving tortoises are all skillful hunters. Their mouths, including jaws, teeth, and tongue, are usually the most dangerous parts.

The **Nile crocodile** is a fearsome hunter. It lies in wait along riverbanks and attacks unsuspecting mammals when they come to drink. It drags them into the water and eats them.

*Nile crocodile
and Wildebeest*

Snakes' jaws are very elastic and usually have sharp teeth. These mobile jaws allow the **egg-eating snake** to swallow eggs several times larger than its own head, and the python to gulp down an entire gazelle.

Chameleons have two special features for hunting. They can turn their large eyes independently to increase the area they control and the accuracy with which they can strike.

15

They use their long, elastic tongue to flick at insects and spiders. Their tongue has sticky mucus on the tip so prey can't escape.

Common chameleon

SNAKES

Only one-third of all snakes are venomous. The venom, produced by glands in the head, passes into the front fangs from where it is injected into the prey or enemy. Pythons, boas, and anacondas suffocate their prey by wrapping their body around the victim.

The **African spitting cobra** is a poisonous snake that can strike from far away. The deadly liquid is squirted at an enemy or prey from up to 10 feet (3 m) away.

African spitting cobra

The **coral snake** has a particularly strong venom. It can kill a human being. Scientists think the coral snake's bright coloring serves as a warning to predators, reminding them how dangerous it is.

Coral snake

Anaconda and alligator

The huge **anaconda** kills its prey by suffocation. Coiling its long body around the prey, it squeezes until the animal can no longer breathe. It eats its victims whole.

REPRODUCTION

Nearly all modern reptiles lay eggs from which their young hatch. A few reptiles give birth to live young. Reptiles, including most aquatic species, nearly always lay eggs or give birth on land.

Turtle eggs and hatchlings

Redbelly snakes

Baby **redbelly snakes** of North America grow inside their mother's body. They are already about 4 inches (10 cm) long when they hatch.

Many **sea turtles** lay their eggs in deep nests they dig in the sand. The hatchlings emerge from the sand and hurry toward the sea. Many are eaten by birds.

Nests and eggs

Reptile eggs have soft, leathery shells. The shells are porous so the babies inside can breathe. The number of eggs laid varies from one to two hundred, depending on the species. They are usually laid in nests prepared by the females or hidden under vegetation.

TRANSFORMATIONS

Young reptiles usually grow bigger as they get older, but they don't change their physical appearance; hatchlings look just as they will as adults, only smaller. Snakes, crocodiles, and lizards renew their scaly skins from time to time.

Snakes regularly shed their skin. The old one gradually loosens, and the snake crawls out of it. A fresh, bright skin is ready underneath. This is called molting.

Four-lined snake

The **green lizard** is a large European species that grows up to 14 inches (35 cm) long, half of which is tail. When threatened by a predator, it can detach its tail, which continues to wriggle and distract the predator. The tail grows back again slowly.

Male green lizard

Turtle hatchlings, such as the one shown here riding on its mother's back, look just as they will when they are fully grown. Their shells become stronger and the colors change, but they provide protection from the time the babies hatch.

European pond turtles

BLENDING IN

The colors and patterns of many reptiles' skins and shells blend in so well with their surroundings that they are almost invisible. This helps them escape the notice of predators and allows them to hunt without being seen by prey.

The **chameleon** can change color to blend in with any environment. It can even resemble a leaf, making it harder to detect.

Common chameleon

Many snakes lie in wait for prey with their body coiled around tree branches. They are often almost invisible against the background foliage. The **yellow snake** shown here is very hard to see against the yellow fruit of the oil palm.

Yellow snake

TYPES OF REPTILES

Scientists divide reptiles into five groups: crocodilians, turtles and tortoises, snakes, lizards, and tuatara. The last group is the smallest. It contains just one species — the tuatara. Lizards make up the largest group. There are about 3,000 different lizard species.

American banded gecko

The **tuatara** is a living fossil. It descends from a group of reptiles that lived on Earth 135 million years ago. Today, it is found only on islands near New Zealand.

Tuatara

Geckos are small lizards that are active mainly at night. They feed on insects, birds, and some small mammals. The male gecko makes noises that sound like its name by clicking its tongue against the roof of its mouth. It is the only lizard that can vocalize.

Gecko feet

Almost all geckos can run up and down steep or vertical surfaces and even zip across ceilings upside-down. The soles of their feet have tiny ridges that help them grip the tiniest irregularities in the surface over which they are moving.

REPTILES AND DINOSAURS

The first reptiles appeared on Earth over 280 million years ago. Several million years later, reptiles called dinosaurs dominated life on Earth. They all became extinct about 65 million years ago.

Komodo dragon

The **Komodo dragon** is the largest living lizard. It can grow up to 10 feet (3 m) in length. It is an active hunter that attacks and kills prey as large as pigs and deer. It has also been known to kill humans.

Basilisks are a type of lizard that can run in an upright position on their back legs over short distances. They can also scoot across the surface of water.

Green basilisk

About 65 million years ago, **Tyrannosaurus**, the fiercest carnivorous dinosaur that ever inhabited Earth, suddenly died out. So did all the other species of dinosaurs living at that time. This marked the end of the reptile regime.

Tyrannosaurus

GLOSSARY

adapt: to make changes or adjustments in order to survive in a changing environment.

algae: a group of plants that grow in water; algae do not have roots, stems, or leaves.

aquatic: of or relating to water; living or growing in water.

arid: having a very dry climate.

decrease: to become fewer.

descend: to come from a particular line of ancestors or previous generations.

dominate: to be present in great numbers in the environment in a certain time or place.

emerge: to appear or come into view.

environment: the surroundings in which plants, animals, and other organisms live.

excess: more than is needed.

excrete: to get rid of waste or unwanted substance from the body.

extinct: no longer living.

ferocious: savage; brutal.

glands: organs in the body that make and release substances such as sweat, tears, saliva, and poison.

irregularities: tiny bumps or ridges that roughen a surface so it is not perfectly smooth.

marine: of or related to the sea.

mobile: able to move or be moved freely.

mucus: a slippery secretion that protects some cell layers.

perch: a roost for a bird, such as a tree branch.

porous: having tiny holes.

predators: animals that kill and eat other animals.

prey: animals that are hunted and killed for food by other animals.

regime: period of domination.

scales: small, thin, plate-like pieces that overlap to cover fish and reptiles.

slither: to slip or slide along, as snakes do.

snout: protruding nose and jaw of an animal.

species: animals or plants that are closely related and often similar in behavior and appearance. Members of the same species are capable of breeding together.

temperate zone: the regions between the tropics north to the Arctic Circle and south to the Antarctic Circle. These regions typically have mild temperatures and moderate humidity.

transformation: a change in form or appearance.

tropical: belonging to the tropics, or the region centered on the equator and lying between the Tropic of Cancer (23.5 degrees north of the equator) and the Tropic of Capricorn (23.5 degrees south of the equator). This region is typically very hot and humid.

venomous: poisonous. Only one-third of all snakes are venomous.

vertical: straight up and down.

vibrations: quivering or trembling motions.

vocalize: to make sounds in the throat; to speak.

ACTIVITIES

1. Make and then play your own card game! Collect some old magazines that have lots of animal pictures. Cut out fifteen pictures of different kinds of reptiles. Cut out five or more pictures of animals that prey on these reptiles, such as eagles, other reptiles, or humans. If you want pictures from a library book, ask someone to help you photocopy them, then color the black-and-white copies with crayons. Paste all your pictures on 3" x 5" index cards. Two to four people can play the card game. Deal all the cards to the players. Each player takes a turn putting one of his or her cards face up in the middle of the table. The player who puts down the card of a reptile enemy can pick up both predator and prey cards. When all the cards have been played, the player who picked up the most cards wins.

2. Pet shops often sell small green chameleons. They make interesting pets. Find out how to care for them, and either borrow one for a while from a friend, or get one for yourself. See if you can take your chameleon with you to different places; be sure to handle your pet gently. What other kinds of reptiles do people keep as pets?

3. Visit a zoo and see how many different kinds of reptiles it has. In what part of the world do these reptiles live in the wild? What do they eat in their natural habitat, and what do they eat in the zoo? Does this zoo try to breed its reptiles? What do the zoo people do with the young? Many zoos have people on staff to answer the questions visitors have.

BOOKS AND VIDEOS

Amazing Crocodiles and Other Reptiles. Mary Ling
(Knopf Books for Young Readers)

FANGS! series. Eric Ethan (Gareth Stevens)

Frogs, Toads, Lizards, and Salamanders. Nancy W. Parker
and Joan R. Wright (Morrow)

*I Wonder Why Snakes Shed Their Skins and Other Questions
About Reptiles.* (Larousse Kingfisher Chambers)

Look Out for Turtles! Melvin Berger (HarperCollins)

Reptiles. (AIMS Media video)

Reptiles. Jenny Markert (Child's World)

Reptiles: A First Film. (Phoenix/BFA Films and Video)

Reptiles Are Interesting. (Phoenix/BFA Films and Video)

Roaring Reptiles. D. M. Souza (Lerner Group)

Sea Turtles. Frank Staub (Lerner Group)

Snakes and How They Live. (AIMS Media video)

Snakes, Salamanders, and Lizards. D. Burns (NorthWord)

The World of Reptiles. Darlyne Murawski (Newbridge)

World's Weirdest Reptiles. M. L. Roberts (Troll)

WEB SITES

www.acmepet.com/reptile/library/index.html

www.olcommerce.com/terra/reptile.html

www.yahooligans.com/Science_and_Oddities/Animals/
Alligators_and_Crocodiles/

INDEX